s for all ages

the
Yorkshire
Dales

Compiled by
Dennis and Jan Kelsall

Mapping sourced from Ordnance Survey

Acknowledgements

The authors thank the staff of the Yorkshire Dales National Park Authority for their valuable help.

Text: Dennis and Jan Kelsall
Photography: Dennis and Jan Kelsall
Editorial: Ark Creative (UK) Ltd.
Design: Ark Creative (UK) Ltd.

© Crimson Publishing, a division of Crimson Business Ltd

 This product includes mapping data licensed from Ordnance Survey ® with the permission of the Controller of Her Majesty's Stationery Office. © Crown Copyright 2006. All rights reserved. Licence number 100017593. Ordnance Survey, the OS symbol and Pathfinder are registered trademarks and Explorer, Landranger and Outdoor Leisure are trademarks of the Ordnance Survey, the national mapping agency of Great Britain.

ISBN: 978-0-7117-1601-8

While every care has been taken to ensure the accuracy of the route directions, the publishers cannot accept responsibility for errors or omissions, or for changes in details given. The countryside is not static: hedges and fences can be removed, field boundaries can be altered, footpaths can be rerouted and changes in ownership can result in the closure or diversion of some concessionary paths. Also, paths that are easy and pleasant for walking in fine conditions may become slippery, muddy and difficult in wet weather, while stepping stones across rivers and streams may become impassable.

If you find an inaccuracy in either the text or maps, please write to Crimson Publishing at the address below.

First published 2001
by Jarrold Publishing
Revised and reprinted 2006.

This edition first published in Great Britain 2008 by Crimson Publishing, a division of:
Crimson Business Ltd
Westminster House, Kew Road
Richmond, Surrey, TW9 2ND
www.totalwalking.co.uk

Printed in Singapore. 4/08

A catalogue record for this book is available from the British library.

Front cover: Langstrothdale
Previous page: Climbing back from Arkle Beck into Reeth (Walk 17)

Contents

Keymap

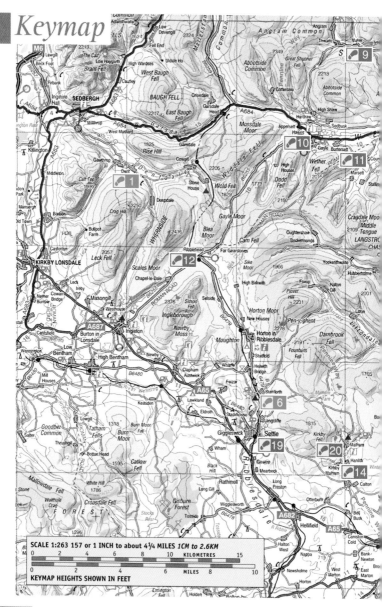

SCALE 1:263 157 or 1 INCH to about 4¼ MILES *1CM to 2.6KM*

KILOMETRES

MILES

KEYMAP HEIGHTS SHOWN IN FEET

Introduction

The routes and information in this book have been devised specifically with families and children in mind. All the walks include points of interest as well as a question to provide an objective.

If you, or your children, have not walked before, choose from the shorter walks for your first outings. The purpose is not simply to get from A to B but to enjoy an exploration, which may be just a steady stroll in the countryside.

The walks are graded by length and difficulty, but few landscapes are truly flat, so even shorter walks may involve some ascent. Details are given under Route Features in the first information box for each route. But the precise nature of the ground underfoot will depend on recent weather conditions. If you do set out on a walk and discover the going is harder than you expected, or the weather has deteriorated, do not be afraid to turn back. The route will always be there another day, when you are fitter or the children are more experienced or the weather is better.

Bear in mind that the countryside also changes. Landmarks may disappear, gates may become styles, rights of way may be altered. However, with the

The Ribblehead Viaduct remains a tribute to its Victorian builders (Walk 12)

aid of this book and its maps you should be able to enjoy many interesting family walks in the countryside.

The Yorkshire Dales

For the walker, coming to the Yorkshire Dales for the first time is like an initial chance meeting with a person

Neat walls and laithes

who later becomes a lifelong friend: there is an immediate rapport, but also a sense of something much deeper that will take time to unearth. And like people, the Dales have many characteristics that alter day by day, changing with the seasons, the weather and the hour. As with a friend, a lifetime can never be enough to discover all.

High moors and gentle valleys

Set fairly in the middle of the great Pennine chain that sweeps through Northern England, the Yorkshire Dales has a quality not found elsewhere. It is a distinction reflected in its people, their traditions and the villages in which they live, and is a product, at least in part, of the unique landscape. Although the region encompasses vast expanses of high, lonely moor and has many respectable hills worthy of ascent, it is the intricate web of gentle valleys that gives the area its name, the Dales.

Uplift and erosion have created a highly varied landscape, full of interest and beauty, founded predominantly on limestone. From wet upland bog to lush riverside meadows, green valleys to stark defiles, and grey cliffs to verdant woodland, every walk offered here unfolds as a changing vista.

The Ice Age has been crucial in moulding the landscape, creating the extensive limestone pavements that appear in the south west. Even in retreat, the ice left its mark, in drumlins, moraines and strange erratic boulders, stranded as aliens in a foreign country. And the massive torrents of water, released by melting ice, cut rocky ravines on a scale irreconcilable with the becks now flowing at their base. The process continues, and the many spectacular waterfalls, so often the focus for a walk, remain a testament to its power. Rainfall has a more subtle action, imperceptibly dissolving the limestone along its cracks and fissures to create enigmatic features that characterise limestone country: grikes, gaping holes and disappearing rivers – the portals to a mysterious world below ground.

Changing ways of life

Farming has ever been the mainstay of economic activity in the Dales, and a major instrument of man's own contribution to the moulding of the landscape. Thousands of miles of drystone wall divide the wide valleys into a patchwork of neat fields, whilst the hillsides are scoured by an innumerable population of nibbling sheep. Mining for lead and zinc ore as well as coal and quarrying for stone have been important industries too. Quarrying still continues in places. But after its heyday, during the late 18th and 19th centuries, the output from these remote workings was unable to match imported metal prices. The gaunt remains of the mines and smelt mills now lie derelict amongst the high moors, a place to pause, take out your flask and let your imagination free.

Ever since the first Norse settlers introduced sheep to the area, textiles have played a significant role. In medieval times, huge tracts of open land were put to sheep runs by their monastic owners, generating a vast income for the abbeys from the export of wool and turning many of the villages into busy market centres. Spinning and weaving developed as cottage industries, and as the factory system emerged, the fast flowing rivers were harnessed to power mills. More important in some areas was knitting, often undertaken by every member within a community. However, the advent of steam power and machinery took the work away.

Yet, as one door closed another opened as the railway heralded the dawn of a new industry, tourism. The beauties of the landscape had already been extolled by early Victorian artists and poets and now, for the first time, cheap, convenient transport brought them in reach of ordinary people, who began flocking to the Dales as both day-trippers and holiday makers. As today, many came simply as sightseers, but the more energetic and adventurous established a tradition of exploratory rambling for which the region is so popular today.

Network of paths and trackways

Although apparently remote, even before the coming of the turnpikes in the 18th century, the area was well served by a network of paths and trackways. From man's earliest incursions, tracks snaked into the hills and, as settlements spread into the valleys after the Roman period, so did the paths. The medieval period saw a proliferation of communication, with new routes springing up connecting the monastic houses with their extensive estates, remote granges and markets. Added to this were the

Stone cottages at Middlesmoor (Walk 13)

tracks established by drovers, bringing Scottish cattle to English markets. Many traditional routes remain, the basis for the network of footpaths and bridleways enjoyed by today's walkers, and with over 1,100 miles (1,770km) criss-crossing the hills and dales of the National Park, there is no lack of opportunity to explore in the finest way – on foot.

The walks in this book are suggested as an introduction to the many aspects of this wonderful area and to help you explore some of the rich legacy that nature, history, occupation and industry have imparted. From the gentle landscape and wooded valleys of the lower dales to the splendid isolation and stark beauty of the encompassing hills, there is something new to explore at every turn. In the villages too there is much to see, with the buildings often reflecting different periods of their prosperity. Many have small museums that interpret the area's natural and social histories, and do not forget to look around the churches, which in many ways have maintained the spirit of village life over the centuries.

1 *Around Dent*

START Dent
DISTANCE 3 miles (4.8km)
TIME 1½ hours
PARKING Car park in village (Pay and Display)
ROUTE FEATURES Steep climb at beginning of walk; a stream crossing; awkward stiles

Although beginning steeply up Flinter Gill, the ascent is soon accomplished and the effort compensated with stunning views to the Howgills. After wandering between hillside farms, the route ambles along the banks of the Dee. Back in Dent, visit St Andrew's Church or look for the massive block of granite commemorating the Victorian geologist Adam Sedgwick.

In the 18th century, Dent prospered from both farming and quarrying, and just about everybody contributed to the other main industry, **knitting**. Not a moment was lost to the task, with social groups gathering every evening to gossip, read aloud and tell stories, all to the accompaniment of clicking needles.

Begin along a lane opposite the car park entrance beside Dent Memorial Hall and keep ahead past the village green (signposted Flinter Gill). The climbing lane becomes a stone track as it leaves the village, where it steepens alongside a wooded gorge, once a packhorse route to Lancaster.

A Just beyond a gate by a barn, part way up, bear left off the track onto a faint path, which leads into the gully. Tumbling over wide, flat slabs, the stream is easily crossed with care to a path, which climbs the opposite bank to a stile. Walk

> **?** *The floor of St Andrew's chancel is paved in Dent marble. What is embedded in the stone?*

PUBLIC TRANSPORT Bus service from Sedburgh
REFRESHMENTS Stone Close Tea Shop, George and Dragon, and Sun Inn (bar meals with children's menu) in Dent, picnic area beside car park
PUBLIC TOILETS Adjoining the car park
CHILDREN'S PLAY AREA By the village green, passed early in the walk
ORDNANCE SURVEY MAPS Explorer OL2 (Yorkshire Dales – Southern & Western areas), Landranger 98 (Wensleydale & Upper Wharfedale)

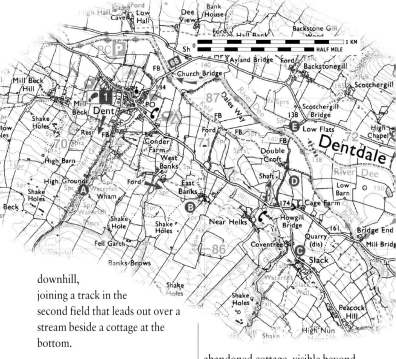

downhill,
joining a track in the
second field that leads out over a
stream beside a cottage at the
bottom.

Immediately past the cottage, turn
right at a sign pointing across the
fields towards Coventree. On
reaching the third field, make for a
gated stile in the top
wall, just beyond a
barn. From there, a
hedged path drops
to a junction above a
cottage, West Banks.
Ignore the crossing
track, instead pass
through a pinch-stile
in the opposite wall
and walk across
towards an

The Adam Sedgwick memorial

abandoned cottage, visible beyond
the trees ahead.

Carry on beside a barn to a narrow
stile and continue over the fields to
the next farm, East
Banks **B**. Crossing
wall-stiles, bypass
the farm buildings
to the right and
carry on across the
fields towards yet
another farm, Near
Helks.

Approaching the
farm, bear left to a

gate into the farmyard and on along a track past the farmhouse. Where the way bends left, walk ahead towards cottages at Far Helks and then bear left behind them. Cross the field beyond, dropping to go over a stile in its far boundary by some trees and on above a wooded gully to a gate. Through the trees, a footbridge crosses the head of the gorge, beyond which the way lies through a gate and along a track out to a lane at Coventree.

One of the loveliest churches in the area, St Andrew's still retains **box pews**, identified with the families who occupied them. The pulpit was once a fine Jacobean three-decker affair and the nearby master's desk came from the village school.

C Walk left to a junction and cross to a track beside a cottage (signposted Double Croft Lane). Follow that down to Double Croft Farm, but instead of turning in, go through a gate ahead along the continuation of the track to the River Dee.

D Unfortunately, the lower track is subject to flooding and may be impassable. A solution is planned, but in the meantime, *it may be necessary to detour over a stile on the right, opposite the entrance to Double Croft Farm. Then, walk beside the right-hand wall to Deepdale Beck, turn left and follow it down to the Dee, continuing ahead to rejoin the main route.*

E Head downstream beside the Dee. Eventually, the way parts company with the river, crossing a field to a bridge spanning Keld Beck. Once over, follow the stream right to its confluence with the Dee below Church Bridge and there climb onto a lane.

Dent lies only a short distance to the left. In the village, follow the lane around to the right in front of the church to return to the car park. ●

Above Flinter Gill

Askrigg to Mill Gill Falls

START Askrigg
DISTANCE 2¼ miles (3.6km)
TIME 1½ hours
PARKING In front of St Oswald's Church
ROUTE FEATURES Narrow stiles; field paths may be muddy

2

A short climb above Askrigg takes the route onto an old moorland lane, giving magnificent views across Herriot's Wensleydale. The way back crosses Mill Gill above the falls, dropping into the gorge lower down for a spectacular view of the cascade. The final section follows a beautiful woodland path above the river before returning to the village.

Leave the village along Mill Lane, behind St Oswald's Church. Twisting between cottages, look for the Old School House, set back some 100 yds (91m) along on the right, beside which a passage leads to the field behind.

Lying beside the Richmond to Lancaster turnpike and, later, the railway, Askrigg was once an important town with industries that included **dying**, **spinning**, **hand-knitting** and **clock-making**. Its former prosperity is reflected in St Oswald's Church, the biggest in the dale. The impressive **beamed roof** above its nave is considered to be one of the finest in the county.

? *What was the purpose of the iron ring embedded in the ground by the village cross?*

Bearing right, climb to a stile by a projecting wall corner. Continue in the next field, swinging left alongside its rising wall over the crest of the hill. Cross a stream beyond the bottom wall to a farm track and go left.

A However, instead of recrossing the stream, go right through the right-most of two adjacent gates and into a widening pasture.

PUBLIC TRANSPORT Bus service between Leyburn and Hawes
REFRESHMENTS Sykes's House tearoom, Crown Inn and King's Arms (bar meals) in Askrigg
PUBLIC TOILETS Beside the main road down the hill from Askrigg
ORDNANCE SURVEY MAPS Explorer OL30 (Yorkshire Dales – Northern & Central areas), Landranger 98 (Wensleydale & Upper Wharfedale)

Field barns, or laithes, in Wensleydale

across the valley and of Bainbridge's Roman fort. After ⅓ mile (536m), turn through a double gate on the left signed to Helm. Passing a Nissen-style barn, head down and around the bottom of a rough enclosure. Where the track later bends into a farmyard at Leas House, leave and walk ahead through a gate.

Follow the left-hand wall up the fields, emerging through a final stile at the top onto Low Straights Lane.

The route (signposted Askrigg via Mill Gill) follows a wall before dropping left to a footbridge over the beck. Climb to a stile in the wall above the opposite bank and

B To the left, a gentle climb soon levels, giving an excellent view

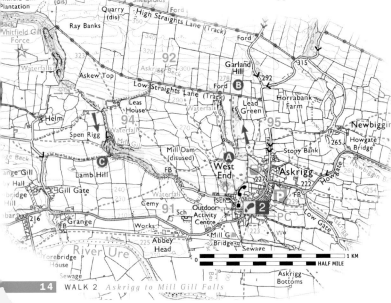

continue down the wooded gorge before eventually emerging into a meadow. Carry on to another stile on the left, cross a footbridge spanning the gill, and then follow the stream to the former mill.

Twisting beneath an aqueduct that supplied water to the wheel, the way emerges into the corner of a field. A flagged path then leads to a final stile onto a track, there turn left back to the village.

when through it, turn left down the fields. After a couple of stiles, the way enters woodland above the gorge and drops past an old lime kiln to a junction. A path leads left, back to the base of the falls.

C Return to the junction and

Sykes's House in Askrigg

3 *Aysgarth Falls*

START Aysgarth Falls National Park Information Centre

DISTANCE 2¼ miles (3.6km)

TIME 1 hour

PARKING Car park at National Park Information Centre (Pay and Display)

ROUTE FEATURES Paths through woodland and across fields may be muddy

After passing Aysgarth's Middle and Lower Falls, the walk rises across open farmland above the Ure to give excellent views across Wensleydale. After returning through the ancient woodland of Freeholders' Wood, it is only a short walk to the Upper Falls and, nearby is the Yorkshire Carriage Museum and St Andrew's Church.

Below Aysgarth village, the **River Ure** falls through a narrow, wooded gorge, dropping 200ft (61m) in only ½ mile (800m). After heavy rain, the river thunders in a boiling torrent over successive limestone steps, the famous falls.

 Leave the car park by the Information Centre along a short footpath beside the road to the right. Then, cross to a gate into Freeholders' Wood. Bearing right, follow a path (signposted Middle and Lower Falls), shortly passing steps on the right to a viewing platform above the Middle Falls.

After leaving the woods through a gate, continue past the return route from the Lower Falls to a gate at

? *Where is there an explanation of how the waterfalls were formed?*

the bottom. Descend a wooded slope towards the river, taking the right branch where the path splits, to emerge on a rocky bank above the Lower Falls.

Just upstream, a marked path returns through the trees to the

PUBLIC TRANSPORT Bus services between Leyburn and Hawes and from Leeds

REFRESHMENTS Coppice Coffee Shop in Information Centre and Mill Race Tea Shop next to Carriage Museum, picnic area by Upper Falls

PUBLIC TOILETS Adjoining visitor centre

ORDNANCE SURVEY MAPS Explorer OL30 (Yorkshire Dales –Northern & Central areas), Landranger 98 (Wensleydale & Upper Wharfedale)

main path. Turn right as if to repeat the loop, but after 20 yds (18m), bear left onto a grass path to Castle Bolton and Redmire **A**. At the end of a fence on the left, cross a stile into an open field.

Aysgarth's Upper Falls

Heading slightly left, walk up towards Hollins House Farm in the middle distance. Eventually joining a track, leave the field through a gate and continue up to the farm. Go right past the barns and farmhouse to follow a surfaced track across the fields beyond.

After 300 yds (274m), at a cattle-grid **B**,

cross a stile on the left into a rough enclosure, once a railway trackbed. Go right, to the corner, and then, beneath a sign to Aysgarth, turn left alongside a fence.

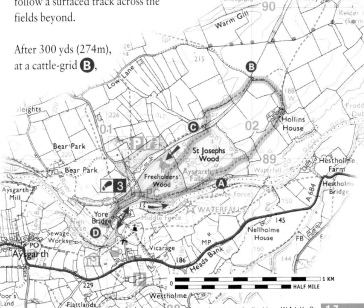

Leaving established natural woodland on the route in late autumn

At the end of the fence, through a gated squeeze-stile, walk ahead across a large pasture. On reaching the far side, turn left down a dipping track and beneath a bridge through the embankment, where a stile leads into St Joseph's Wood.

C Bear right at a marker just ahead and follow a winding path between the young trees towards Aysgarth. Shortly, cross a stile into Freeholders' Wood and continue

on a descending path. At the bottom, leave through the gate by which you first entered the wood and turn right, back to the car park.

The Upper Falls are easily reached along a short footpath from the far end of the car park. There is a small charge, but the meadow overlooking the falls is a fine spot for a picnic **D**.

The fine church of St Andrew's above the falls used to serve the whole of upper Wensleydale and reputedly has the **largest graveyard in the country**. Amongst its treasures is a beautifully **carved and gilded rood-screen**, brought from Jervaulx Abbey at the Dissolution.

So called because medieval freeholders enjoyed '**estover**', the right to gather wood, Freeholders' Wood is a remnant of the broad-leaved forest that once filled the valley. It is once again managed in the traditional method of coppicing, where the trees are periodically cut back to a stool, thus providing a regular supply of small timber.

Burton Force and Morpeth Scar

4

START West Burton

DISTANCE 2¾ miles (4.4km)

TIME 1½ hours

PARKING Roadside parking around village green

ROUTE FEATURES Sustained climb during early part of walk

Although involving a stiff climb early on, the walk is not difficult and the height gained affords magnificent views across Bishopdale and Wensleydale. The way back lies along an old track, Morpeth Gate, and then a woodland path, to allow you a second view of the splendid waterfall before returning to the village.

Like many Dales villages, the cottages of West Burton cluster around its **village green**, but this must be one of the largest in the whole country. The **village cross** is also unusual, an octagonal, stepped base topped by a pyramidal cap. It was only built in 1820 but probably replaced a much earlier market cross, for a large weekly market was once held on the site.

Leave the bottom, northern corner of the village green by a track (signposted Morpeth Gate, Cote Bridge), which leads past Mill House to the waterfall. On the opposite bank, the path climbs steps out of the gorge and then follows a fenced field path. Keep going up the subsequent field, continuing beyond the end of a wall to cross a stile into the corner of Barrack Wood, ahead to the left.

A Climb alongside its perimeter fence to a squeeze-stile in the top wall. Carry on up a scrubby bank and over a fence-stile at the top and once there bear right to a broken stile in the opposite wall.

? *What is the distinctive feature of a packhorse bridge?*

PUBLIC TRANSPORT Bus service between Leyburn and Hawes

REFRESHMENTS Fox and Hounds at West Burton

PUBLIC TOILETS Nearest public toilets at Aysgarth Falls

ORDNANCE SURVEY MAPS Explorer OL30 (Yorkshire Dales – Northern & Central areas), Landranger 98 (Wensleydale & Upper Wharfedale)

Avoiding a direct ascent of the steep slope, the path rises first left and then right to reach a stile in the top wall.

With the main climb now over, walk away bearing slightly right across the open moorland. Make for a large cairn, which soon comes into view below the far wall, where you will find a stone track **B**. Turn left along it to Morpeth Scar.

Swaledale sheep, bred for the hills

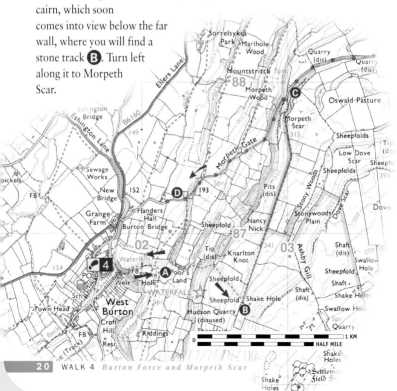

Gently losing height, the track affords fantastic views left across the foot of Bishopdale and ahead across Wensleydale to Bolton Castle. After crossing a ladder-stile, the descent gradually steepens, eventually dropping to a junction with another track, Morpeth Gate.

C Turn left (signposted West Burton and Barrack Wood), the way shortly becoming quite wooded. After about ½ mile (800m), where the track curves right to leave the trees, go through a gate on the left beneath a large holly tree onto a path to Barrack Wood and West Burton **D**. Undulating under the trees, the way leads through a couple of gates, eventually returning to the stile by which you originally entered the wood.

Retrace your outward steps across the fields and back down past the waterfall to return to the village. ●

West Burton's village green is one of the largest in England

5 Redmire to Castle Bolton

START Redmire
DISTANCE 3 miles (4.8km)
TIME 1½ hours plus time to visit castle
PARKING Around village square in Redmire
ROUTE FEATURES Field paths may be muddy

The pretty villages of Redmire and Castle Bolton are linked by this pleasant and easy lowland walk, which wanders Wensleydale's rolling green pastures. The highlight is a visit to the imposing and substantial remains of Bolton Castle, which was built in the 14th century and endures today as a spectacular landmark from miles around.

Raised in 1379 by Richard Scrope, Chancellor to Richard II, **Bolton Castle** was both a defence against the Scots and a comfortable residence befitting his station. Mary Queen of Scots was imprisoned here in 1568, but she was well treated by the local nobility, many of whom adhered to the 'old faith'. After falling to the Parliamentarians during the civil wars, the castle was abandoned but it remains a magnificent building and there is much to see inside.

Leave the village towards Grinton and Reeth but, immediately, turn left before a telephone box and follow a winding street between cottages and past the King's Arms. Beyond the last cottage, go through a waymarked squeeze-stile on the right and diagonally cross the field to leave its far corner.

Turn right to follow a lane into the Dales National Park. Where the road then bends right in front of Low Bolton Farm, fork left onto a

? What tells you when street lighting arrived in Redmire?

PUBLIC TRANSPORT Bus service from Leyburn
REFRESHMENTS King's Arms and Bolton Arms in Redmire (bar meals), tearoom at Bolton Castle
PUBLIC TOILETS Adjacent to the car park at Bolton Castle
ORDNANCE SURVEY MAPS Explorer OL30 (Yorkshire Dales – Northern & Central areas), Landranger 98 (Wensleydale & Upper Wharfedale)

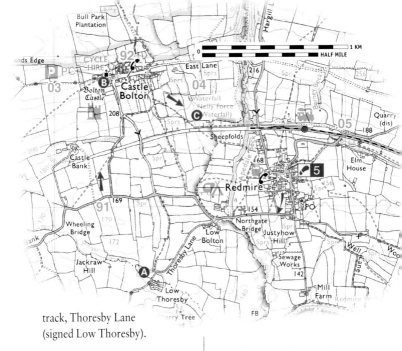

track, Thoresby Lane
(signed Low Thoresby).

A After ⅓ mile (536m), where the track turns left to ford a stream, climb to a stile on the right and on into a field. Turning right, walk away from the stream. Cross another stile at the top right corner into the next field and continue in the same direction up the subsequent field to emerge onto a lane at the top.

Although the lane opposite offers the most direct way to Castle Bolton, a more interesting route lies along the road to the left. After 350 yds (320m), turn right onto an old hedged track (signposted to Castle Bolton).

Apedale Beck, behind Redmire village

Beyond a stile, the track continues up the field edge and, across more stiles, over the abandoned Wensleydale Railway. A drive from a cottage there leads to a lane, the village is then a short walk up to the left.

B At the junction, go left to the castle entrance, or, to continue the walk, turn right into the village (signposted Redmire and Reeth). Towards the far end, where the lane bends left, go ahead along a track towards cottages, but then immediately turn right onto another track (signposted to Redmire), through gates into the field behind.

Carry on into the second field, but 70 yds (64m) down, go through a stile in the wall on the left. Walk away, bearing right to another stile in the far corner and continue in the same direction across the next two fields.

C After crossing a stream, bear left along the edges of successive rough fields, keeping the abandoned railway line on your right. Shortly, beside an embankment, go ahead, crossing a footbridge over Apedale Beck and then out to a lane beyond.

Turn right and follow the lane beneath a railway bridge back to Redmire. At the bottom, bend left past the village's second pub, the Bolton Arms, and carry on to the village green.

Bolton Castle

Stainforth to Catrigg Force

START Stainforth

DISTANCE 2¼ miles (3.6km)

TIME 1½ hours

PARKING Car park in village (Pay and Display)

ROUTE FEATURES Awkward stiles; a sustained climb at the beginning of the walk

6

A splendid walk over hillsides above the Ribble to a dramatic foss on Stainforth Beck, Catrigg Force. From this picturesque spot, where the stream tumbles merrily into an arboreal gully, the return is down an old, stony track that gives grand views towards the distant moors of Bowland to the west.

From the car park, turn right into the village and then go right again over a bridge across Stainforth Beck. Opposite the Craven Heifer, walk left up a side lane and, at the top, turn right and then immediately left onto a track between some cottages (signposted Winskill). Over a stile, walk on into a field, crossing to a gate in its far, upper corner.

? *What is a heifer?*

The **Craven Heifer** is one of several pubs in the district bearing the name. It celebrates a young cow bred in Gargrave at the beginning of the 19th century and which weighed over a ton. The Craven Bank even used its image on a bank-note issued in 1817.

Through the gate, keep going beside the left-hand fence of a long enclosure until you reach a kissing-gate. From there, a stepped path climbs, rather steeply, up the wooded bank of Stainforth Scar. Emerging from the trees at the top, go over a stile into a rough field and carry on to cross a ladder-stile

PUBLIC TRANSPORT Bus service from Settle

REFRESHMENTS Craven Heifer (children welcome) and picnic area in Stainforth

PUBLIC TOILETS Adjoining car park

ORDNANCE SURVEY MAPS Explorer OL2 (Yorkshire Dales – Southern & Western areas), Landranger 98 (Wensleydale & Upper Wharfedale)

on the far wall. There, bear left towards a farm, Lower Winskill, passing over another stile and through a gate to reach the farmyard.

The open moors rise steeply behind Stainforth

A Leave through a gate opposite along a gently rising track to Upper Winskill and walk ahead past its entrance, following a wall on the left at the edge of open moor. Then, over a ladder-stile, follow a field track down

Catrigg Force is perhaps one of the prettiest waterfalls in the Dales. The beck drops abruptly in two steps through a narrow cleft in the rock, falling into a deep pool at the head of a wooded gorge, 60ft (18m) below. The fall is variously referred to as 'foss' and 'force', both derivations of the old Norse *fors* and a reminder of early settlers in the Dales.

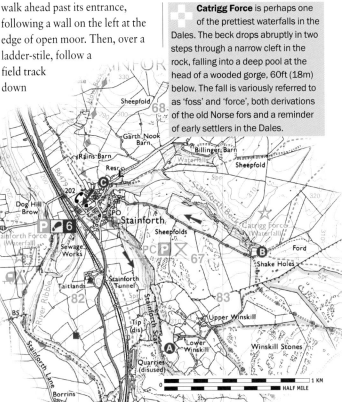

to a junction and turn left into the next field. Continue dropping to leave through a gate at the bottom corner onto the end of a walled track. From a gate immediately on the right, a path then leads down to the waterfall and gorge (signposted Catrigg Foss).

B Climb back from the beck to the walled track and turn right, following it down the hill to Stainforth. When you reach the village green **C**, to return to the car park, you can either walk ahead to cross the river by a line of

Meaning 'stony ford', **Stainforth** takes its name from an ancient river crossing, not of Stainforth Beck, crossed here, but of the Ribble, which lies downstream, just to the west. Although not described in the walk, wander down a narrow lane off the main road just north of the village to see **Stainforth Bridge**, a magnificent parapeted packhorse bridge built in 1670 to replace the ford. You will find another stepped waterfall, just downstream.

ancient stepping stones and then past the church or carry on down to the Craven Heifer and the road bridge. ●

Ancient stepping stones at Stainforth

7 Conistone Pie

START Conistone
DISTANCE 3 miles (4.8km)
TIME 1½ hours
PARKING Roadside
parking by Conistone
Bridge and around village
ROUTE FEATURES Wall-
stiles; short and easy
scrambles

A gem of a walk exploring the limestone scenery above Conistone. The climb up a splendid, narrow dry valley is a prelude to a fine hill-top walk above the limestone escarpment of Hill Castles. From Conistone Pie – a descriptively distinctive outcrop – there are magnificent views, which linger on the return to the village, following an old packhorse route.

The earliest cottages in the dale date from the 17th century, when improvements in agricultural practice brought increasing prosperity and the yeomen farmers began rebuilding their wood and lathe houses and barns in stone. The impressive mullioned windows and carved doorway lintels were an expression of their new confidence.

From Conistone Bridge, walk to a junction in the village centre and bear left. Where the lane then bends left, fork right onto a track climbing between cottages across an open green. Go through a gate at the top and on between sheep-pens (signposted to Conistone Dib).

The way ahead rises into a narrowing gorge that penetrates the high ground behind the village. Once containing a stream, its bed is now dry, and the low steps and falls, over which the water once

What do the numbers on top of the signpost in the village mean?

PUBLIC TRANSPORT Bus services from Ilkley and Leeds
REFRESHMENTS Nearby, there is a café at Kilnsey Park and the Tennant's Arms (bar meals with children's portions), a little farther along the road
PUBLIC TOILETS None
ORDNANCE SURVEY MAPS Explorer OL2 (Yorkshire Dales – Southern & Western areas), Landranger 98 (Wensleydale & Upper Wharfedale)

tumbled, remain as an easy scramble. In places, so narrow that both sides can be touched at once, the valley is full of contrasts and, elsewhere, widens to hold a green swathe of grazing at its base.

Follow the old stream bed right to the head of the valley, climbing over a couple of stiles on the way up. At the top, after a third stile, go around to the left above the stream bed and walk on up a short walled track to emerge from the valley through a gate onto the open hillside.

St Mary's Church, Conistone

A Walk ahead, crossing a track, Scot Gate Lane, which drops from the right, continuing on a level grass track below a low scar. The cliff is,

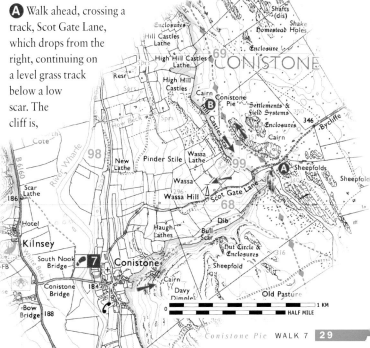

in fact, the edge of an extensive area of limestone pavement above. It is worth making a short detour here to have a look. *However, take care in wet or icy weather, for the rocks can become very slippery.*

The unmistakable outline of Conistone Pie shortly comes into view ahead, to the left of the path beyond a final stile.

The valley's glacial character is unmistakable: a wide, flat bottom contained within abruptly rising sides. For a time, a moraine held a lake in this section of the dale, allowing sediments to collect and so level the plain below.

B After enjoying the view, retrace your steps along the grass path to the junction with Scot Gate Lane and turn right to follow the track down the hillside. After passing a transmitter mast, the lane steepens and there are glimpses into the gorge by which you climbed up. When you reach the lane at the bottom, go left to return to the village, passing the church on the right.

Mastile's Lane climbs steeply away up the opposite side of the valley from the former monastic grange at Kilnsey. Its origins are perhaps Roman, for it was once known as Strete Gate, leading to a Roman camp near Malham Tarn. Climbing on across the moor, it later formed part of a route connecting Fountains Abbey with its estates in Lakeland and was also used by the cattle drovers.

It is claimed that two of the arches along the aisle of **St Mary's Church** were already standing before the Normans arrived in Britain, which bestows it the honour as the oldest building still standing in Craven.

Conistone Dib provides a path onto the hills

Around Burnsall

START Burnsall

DISTANCE 3 miles (4.8km)

TIME 1½ hours

PARKING Car park at edge of village (coin-operated barrier)

ROUTE FEATURES Steep climb along field paths at beginning of walk; narrow suspension bridge

A fine walk from the charming village of Burnsall. After a steep but short climb up still well-defined, Anglian field terraces, the route levels across a rolling hillside, from where there are stunning views across the valley. The return follows a particularly beautiful section of the Wharfe, where it twists unexpectedly below the miniature riverside cliffs of Loup Scar.

Burnsall can claim a real-life Dick Whittington in the 16th-century **William Craven**, who travelled to London to seek his fortune and ended up its Lord Mayor. He never forgot his connections and amongst his gifts to the village was a **free grammar school**. A fine, mullion-windowed building, it still stands beside the church, continuing to serve as the local school.

Walk towards the village and turn right by the Red Lion across the bridge. On the opposite bank, go left through a gap in the parapet (signposted Skuff Road), dropping to a field below. Walk upstream to a ladder-stile in the next field. Then, climb steeply ahead up the hillside, to a gated squeeze-stile in the top wall onto Skuff Road.

A Cross to the field directly opposite and resume the climb (signposted Hartlington and Raikes Road). Over a stile at the top, carry on across the next field to a stile in the far wall (not the ladder-stile in the right-hand corner). Bearing left, walk away on a faint path

How old do you think the suspension bridge across the River Wharfe is?

PUBLIC TRANSPORT Bus services from Ilkley, Wakefield and Reeth

REFRESHMENTS Wharfe View Tea Rooms and Red Lion in Burnsall

PUBLIC TOILETS Adjoining car park

ORDNANCE SURVEY MAPS Explorer OL2 (Yorkshire Dales – Southern & Western areas), Landranger 98 (Wensleydale & Upper Wharfedale)

until, in the third field, you are directed right around the perimeter to a gate opposite South View Farm.

B Instead of leaving the field, continue around its edge to cross a stile and then follow waymarks which guide you left, right and then left again along the edges of successive fields.

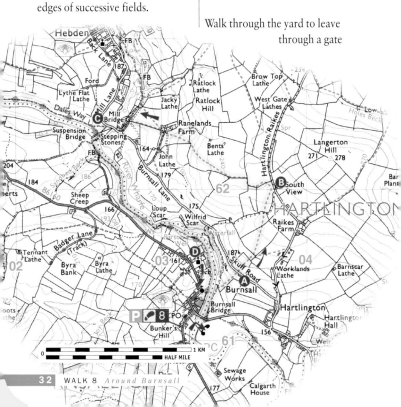

Burnsall from Skuff Road

Eventually, at a signpost part way along a large enclosure, strike off to the right. Pass well left of a field barn and drop to a gate, set back in the bottom wall. Pass through, walk down to the opposite corner of the field and out into a farmyard at Ranelands.

Walk through the yard to leave through a gate

The River Wharfe below Loup Scar

opposite and carry on along the left-hand edge of the field beyond. Ignore a track leaving near the bottom corner, instead crossing a stile just beyond by a cottage in front of you. Walk left down to a lane and there turn right.

C Over Mill Bridge, go through a gate into a field on the left and following a 'Dales Way' sign to Burnsall, cross to another gate in the left-hand wall. A narrow suspension bridge takes the route over the Wharfe.

A clear path to the left follows the riverbank downstream, eventually leading back to Burnsall. You will pass Loup Scar and Wilfrid Scar, where the river runs below small but nevertheless impressive cliffs, and just beyond **D** you can leave the river beside a cottage to visit Burnsall church. You then have the choice of either continuing down the road through the village or resuming the path by the Wharfe to the bridge.

The 7th-century bishop of York, St Wilfrid, is credited with founding the **chapel** here and relics of its ancient past include **Celtic crosses and Viking hog-back tombstones**. There is also a beautiful medieval alabaster panel depicting the Adoration. Perhaps the church's most unusual feature is the centrally pivoted lychgate, which operates more like a turnstile. Nearby, you will also find the **village stocks**, where miscreants were left to cool their heels for a while.

9 *Muker to Ivelet Bridge*

From the intimacy of winding alleyways and charming stone cottages that is Muker, this walk wanders the valley side giving fine views of upper Swaledale. After dropping to the ancient single-arched packhorse bridge at Ivelet, once a resting point on an ancient corpse way, the route returns by the banks of the lovely River Swale.

START Muker
DISTANCE 4½ miles (7.2km)
TIME 2½ hours
PARKING Car park outside village (Pay and Display)
ROUTE FEATURES Short climbs at start and near end of walk; narrow stiles; field paths may be muddy

Sheep-farming has been a mainstay of Muker ever since Norsemen settled here, but **lead-mining** too has been important, perhaps begun during the Roman occupation of Britain. The industry expanded during the 18th and 19th centuries, and many of the village's 'new' cottages date from this period.

Leave the car park beside the bridge over Straw Beck outside Muker, as if to follow the road to Gunnerside. However, immediately bear right onto a track (waymarked Bridleway and Occupation Road). After passing between two barns at the top, the track bends right to dip across a culverted stream. Just beyond, go through the second of two gates on the left.

Generally follow the left-hand wall along the bottom edge of a succession of moorland enclosures. Eventually emerging through a gate at Rash, the route continues

What was the walled enclosure by the car park in Muker used for?

PUBLIC TRANSPORT Bus service from Richmond
REFRESHMENTS Tea shop and inn, the Farmer's Arms (families welcome) in Muker
PUBLIC TOILETS On main street in Muker
ORDNANCE SURVEY MAPS Explorer OL30 (Yorkshire Dales – Northern & Central areas), Landranger 98 (Wensleydale & Upper Wharfedale)

along a track. After passing another farmhouse, drop across a bridge and then turn off right through a gate to climb towards more cottages.

A Immediately before the cottages, pass through a narrow gate into a field on the right and bear left to a wooden stile at the far side. Climb over, follow the wall up to the left, crossing more stiles to enter the corner of a field by a barn. Walk away on a right diagonal and over another stile by the high point of the top wall. There, turn left through a gate and bear right across a final enclosure to emerge onto a lane.

B Go right, but after almost ¼ mile (400m), turn off

through a waymarked gate on the left. Bearing left, walk across towards the corner of Kearton's Wood and on over a stile in the wall just beyond. Bear left along the rim of a deepening wooded

gully above Oxnop Beck descending to a farm at Low Oxnop.

Pass the farm to the right and, immediately beyond the barns, cross a stile on the left into a field. Carry on above the stream, eventually leaving onto a lane beside Oxnop Bridge. Cross the stream and then turn left down a narrower lane to Ivelet Bridge.

C Over the bridge, go through a gate on the left and, for the next mile (1.6km) or so, follow the river upstream across a succession of

An old lane takes the walk out of Muker

Ivelet Bridge carried a packhorse trail across the River Swale

meadows towards Muker. Eventually, as the village comes into view, the way diverges from the river **D**, bearing right across the fields to bypass the Swale's confluence with Straw Beck. Keep going, passing Ramps Holme Farm and then, a little while after, dropping back to the Swale, where there is a bridge across.

St Mary the Virgin is one of the country's few Elizabethan churches and was built as a chapel of ease to save parishioners the long journey to the mother church at Grinton.

Upstream on the opposite bank, ignore a stile on the left, from which a paved path crosses the flood meadows direct to Muker. Instead, continue by the river, over a stile and on to a barn. Immediately past it, turn sharp left onto a grass track that rises up the fields behind. Shortly levelling, it continues through gates as a walled track, eventually being joined by another track to drop into Muker. Walk down through the village to the main lane and turn left, crossing the bridge back to the car park.

10 *Hawes to Hardraw Force*

START Hawes
DISTANCE 4¼ miles (6.8km)
TIME 2¼ hours
PARKING Car park beside Dales Countryside Museum and National Park Information Centre (Pay and Display)
ROUTE FEATURES Narrow stiles; field paths may be muddy

Crossing the Ure's flood meadows onto the valley's northern slopes, this roundabout route to Hardraw offers stunning views across the dale. After visiting the famous waterfall, a spectacular sight following heavy rain, an easy walk leads back across the fields to Hawes. Complete the day by visiting the Dales Countryside Museum or the nearby rope works.

? *Most Yorkshire dales are named after their river, but what is the river here and what gives the dale its name?*

Start by climbing a path beside the toilets from the car park onto Brunt Acres Road and turn right over a bridge away from Hawes. About 100 yds (91m) on, by the entrance to the town's industrial estate, leave over a stile on the left and cut across the fields along a flagged path, rejoining the road at the far side.

Located in Hawes' former railway station, the **Dales Countryside Museum** gives a fascinating insight into Wensleydale life since its colonisation after the retreating glaciers of the last Ice Age. Displays feature many topics showing how man's various activities have shaped the character of the dale, and highlights include a reconstructed lead mine and traditional Dales kitchen.

PUBLIC TRANSPORT Bus services from Kendal, Leyburn and Leeds
REFRESHMENTS Choice of pubs and cafés in Hawes, Simonstone Hall Hotel in Simonstone, and Green Dragon Inn, Shepherd's Kitchen and Cart Horse Tea Room at Hardraw
PUBLIC TOILETS Adjoining visitor centre
CHILDREN'S PLAY AREA Opposite car park
ORDNANCE SURVEY MAPS Explorer OL30 (Yorkshire Dales – Northern & Central areas), Landranger 98 (Wensleydale & Upper Wharfedale)

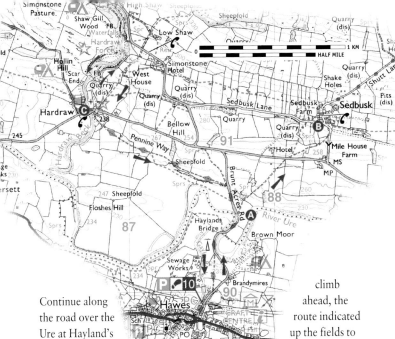

Continue along the road over the Ure at Hayland's Bridge, as far as a stile on the right.

A A sign there directs you diagonally left across the fields towards Sedbusk. Beyond an arched packhorse bridge at the edge of a wood, bear right to climb across more fields, eventually emerging over a stile onto a lane.

Cross right to another stile and

Field enclosures above Hawes

climb ahead, the route indicated up the fields to Sedbusk Lane. Beyond a dip, the way eventually rises again to a stile near the top right corner of the last field, leaving onto the lane.

B Go right, but then immediately cross a stile on the left and walk up to another stile in the left-hand wall. Through that, head away, at times following a fence

Packhorse bridge above Hawes

waymark to walk down the fields to Hardraw.

The path enters the village beside the Green Dragon Inn, through which you actually pass to see the waterfall. It lies behind, at the head of a narrow wooded gorge, and there is a small charge for admission.

C The return route lies over a stile to the right of the Shepherd's Kitchen Café, directly opposite the Green Dragon. A flagged path (signposted Pennine Way to Brunt Acres Road) leads behind the buildings and away across the fields.

line, across a succession of narrow fields towards Simonstone, whose buildings shortly come into view.

Emerging onto a lane, turn left, but then go right along a drive to Simonstone Hall Hotel (signposted Hardraw). Outside the entrance gates, cross a stile on the left into a meadow and turn right beside a low wall. Keep going through two more stiles and then bear left at a

Keep going where the paved way ends, following a wall on the right until, eventually, you emerge onto Brunt Acres Road. Turn right and retrace your steps back to Hawes and the starting point. ●

The flagged paths radiating from many Dales villages are known as '**causeys**' and were laid to ease the journeys of the coal-miners, lead-miners and quarrymen as they walked to and from their work.

Rope-making has been carried out in Hawes since about 1840, with the Outhwaite factory first opening in 1905. Inside you can watch the fascinating process take place, in which fibres are skilfully twisted to produce ropes and cords to suit all manner of purposes.

Around Semer Water

START Semer Water, 2 miles (3.2km) south west of Bainbridge
DISTANCE 3¾ miles (6km)
TIME 2 hours
PARKING Car park at foot of lake (charge)
ROUTE FEATURES Narrow stiles; field paths may be muddy; walk along quiet lane

Fed by rivers rooted in three separate dales, Semer Water owes its existence to a retreating glacier that deposited a moraine across the valley mouth. After following a quiet lane into the valley, the walk crosses the dale to return above the opposite shore, where fields, untouched by modern agricultural practice, have become a haven for plant- and wildlife.

With the lake on your left, follow the lane from the car park over Semer Water Bridge. Just beyond, turn through a gate on the left into woodland above the shore and, following a sign to Marsett Lane, walk ahead, rising beyond the trees beside a wall to a gate. Keep going across the next field to climb a stile over the top fence onto the lane.

To the left, rising gently along the valley, there are delightful views across the lake before you descend to the tiny settlement of Marsett, 1¼ miles (2km) away. **A** Across

Semer Water is all that remains of a huge glacial lake that once filled the valley floor and, along with Malham Tarn, is one of only two significant natural bodies of water within the Dales. The large boulders at the foot of the lake are erratics, brought by the glacier, but are more romantically associated with a battle between the devil and a giant, who hurled them at each other.

? *How many erratic boulders can you find near the car park?*

PUBLIC TRANSPORT Bus service to Bainbridge between Leyburn and Hawes
REFRESHMENTS Nearest at Bainbridge, Corn Mill Tea Room and Rose and Crown (bar meals)
PUBLIC TOILETS Nearest public toilets at Bainbridge
ORDNANCE SURVEY MAPS Explorer OL30 (Yorkshire Dales – Northern & Central areas), Landranger 98 (Wensleydale & Upper Wharfedale)

Marsett Bridge, go left by a telephone box and then keep left in front of the buildings to follow a track beside Marsett Beck (signposted Semer Water and Stalling Busk).

High on the fell above the lane lies **Cam High Road**. Built in the 1st century under Agricola, it ran from the fort at Bainbridge via Ribblehead and Ingleton to Ribchester. The route later became part of the turnpike between Richmond and Lancaster.

(46m) along and continue up its opposite side.

Keep going to a barn, just past which, turn left through a stile. Now, walk away, bearing slightly right and maintaining the same direction across successive fields, gradually gaining height along the valley side. Eventually, the

Shortly, the way diverges from the river to cross the width of the valley. Over Rydale Beck (a footbridge beside the ford gives a dry-shod passage) continue to the next stream, Cragdale Water. **B** There, go over a footbridge on the left into the corner of a rough field and walk away beside a wall on the right. Cross by a stile 50 yds

way is joined by a path from Stalling Busk and continues to a gate leading into a graveyard surrounding a ruined chapel.

A well-known erratic boulder at Semer Water

C Instead of going through the gate, turn right, following the wall into the next field. Continue in the same direction beyond its far end to cross another field, eventually passing into the Semer Water Nature Reserve.

A faint path leads through the reserve and, over a stile at its far side, continues beside a wall above the lake, shortly leading you into the corner of a pasture by a barn. Walk to a stile on its far side and maintain the same direction across the subsequent fields, finally emerging over a ladder-stile onto a lane opposite Low Blean Farm. Turn left and follow it back down to the car park at the foot of the lake.

The **tiny church** was founded in 1603 to serve the scattered communities of this lonely dale. Although rebuilt in 1722, it fell into disuse at the beginning of the 20th century, after St Matthew's Church was built at nearby Stalling Busk.

The Bain, England's shortest river, begins at Semer Water Bridge

12 *Ribblehead Viaduct*

This ramble, which generally follows clear tracks and paths, is one best saved for a fine day, in order to fully enjoy the wild and impressive moorland landscape through which it meanders. Ingleborough and Whernside, the highest of Yorkshire's famous Three Peaks compete for your attention with the Ribblehead Viaduct, a monumental triumph of Victorian engineers.

START Ribblehead
DISTANCE 4½ miles (7.2km)
TIME 2 hours
PARKING Roadside parking areas at Ribblehead
ROUTE FEATURES No difficulties

The **Ribblehead Viaduct**, both for its location and scale, is a tribute to all involved in its construction. Twenty-four arches, the highest standing 165ft (50m) above the ground, and two massive embankments carry the track for ¾ mile (1.2km) across the valley head. It is an impressive sight and one of the great feats of Victorian civil engineering.

A rough path, leaving the road opposite the B6479 at its junction with the B6255, heads across the moor towards the viaduct. There, join a track going right but, where it turns beneath the arches, carry on ahead to climb beside the far embankment. Keep on until you reach the second

? Why is the place called Ribblehead?

accommodation bridge beneath the railway, shortly before the signal-box at Bleamoor Sidings.

A Follow the bridleway through to some cottages at Winterscales, crossing

PUBLIC TRANSPORT Bus and rail services from Skipton and Settle
REFRESHMENTS Station Inn
PUBLIC TOILETS None
ORDNANCE SURVEY MAPS Explorer OL2 (Yorkshire Dales – Southern & Western areas), Landranger 98 (Wensleydale & Upper Wharfedale)

a bridge and a cattle-grid before reaching a junction, beyond the farm. Keep ahead, following the track to the next farm, Ivescar, about ⅓ mile (536m) away.

B Through a gate by a barn, where the track then bends left, bear right over a bridge and then go left in front of the farmhouse. Keep ahead through gates beside a corrugated outbuilding and across the field beyond (signposted Scar End).

After crossing an almost dry stream bed in the middle

of the subsequent field, bear right to a gate by the protruding corner of a wall ahead. Continue in the same direction across more fields to Broadrake, the next farm.

> The railway is only the latest in a **succession of routes** that have climbed through the dale to cross the passes into the neighbouring valleys. Throughout the Dales there is a network of prehistoric trods, Roman roads, monastic tracks and packhorse trails, as well as cattle-drove and turnpike roads, many of which are preserved in today's green lanes, footpaths and bridleways.

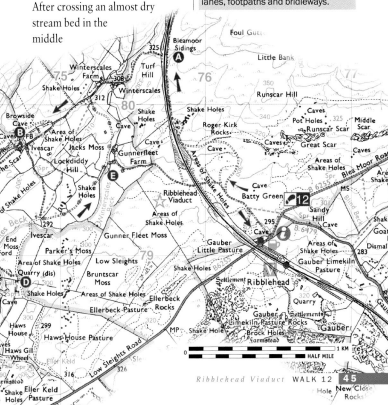

Upstream, Winterscales Beck is full of water, which disappears underground in a **sink** about 100 yds (91m) before reaching the next bridge downstream, the second crossing of it along the route. This, and the equally fascinating phenomenon of **stream resurgence**, is a common feature of the limestone landscape.

During the construction of the railway, a **shanty town** housing some 2,000 workmen grew up near the viaduct on Batty Moss. The work was hazardous so many men lost their lives in accidents, and living conditions in the crude shacks were little better. A smallpox outbreak in 1871 brought disastrous consequences. In all, some 220 people died during the construction, three for every mile of track laid. Many lie buried in the pretty little Church of St Leonard's, at nearby Chapel-le-Dale.

C Turn left in front of the farmhouse and follow a track away. Over a cattle-grid, the track turns right. There, go left along a rough grass track onto the moor and, where that then forks, bear left (signposted Bridleway) to a ladder-stile. After crossing the (usually) dry bed of Winterscales Beck, bend right and then left around higher ground, shortly joining a metalled track as it emerges through a wall.

D Walk left and, after recrossing the waterless beck, bear right at a junction. Follow the track over the fields towards barns at Gunnerfleet Farm and turn right to cross the beck once more.

E Beyond the barns, the track winds towards the viaduct. After passing beneath its towering arches, it leads around to the right, returning you to the road beside the Station Inn back at the starting point. ●

Whernside's slopes rise steeply behind Ivescar

Lofthouse to How Stean Gorge

START Lofthouse
DISTANCE 3¾ miles (6km)
TIME 2 hours plus time to visit How Stean Gorge
PARKING Car park in village
ROUTE FEATURES Paths may be muddy and there is a climb along field paths to Middlesmoor

13

After a pleasant stroll above the River Nidd, a climb to the tiny village of Middlesmoor is rewarded by one of Nidderdale's finest panoramas from St Chad's churchyard. The onward route lies downhill to How Stean Gorge, where you can break your journey to explore its fascinating natural formations. It is then just a short walk along the lane to Lofthouse.

From the car park, turn right and walk up through Lofthouse. Beyond the top of the village, where the lane bends right onto the open moor, go ahead along a track (signposted Nidderdale Way).

Although now seemingly miles from anywhere, a **railway** once passed through Lofthouse, laid at the beginning of the 20th century. It carried construction materials to the reservoirs being built at the head of Nidderdale, but also brought passengers as far as Lofthouse. The line closed in 1936, when Scar House, the second of the two dams, was completed.

? Where can you find health advice on the use of water?

Following the valley side, it undulates easily for about one mile (1.6km), eventually leading into a small yard at Thrope Farm.

A Leave the track, passing around the farm and dropping

PUBLIC TRANSPORT Bus service from Pateley Bridge
REFRESHMENTS Crown Hotels at both Lofthouse and Middlesmoor (bar meals) and cafés at Middlesmoor (Dovenor House) and How Stean Gorge
PUBLIC TOILETS On main road at Lofthouse, by the Crown Hotel at Middlesmoor and at How Stean Gorge
CHILDREN'S PLAY AREA How Stean Gorge Café
ORDNANCE SURVEY MAPS Explorer OL30 (Yorkshire Dales – Northern & Central areas), Landranger 99 (Northallerton & Ripon)

behind to a bridge across the River Nidd. On the opposite bank, climb over the fence on the left and walk away from the bridge along the riverbank.

Half-way along the field, bear right towards a gate in the middle of its end wall, and continue on the same diagonal across the next field. Leave by a stile towards the far corner of its top fence onto a lane.

Walk left 25 yds (23m) to another stile on the right, over which, cut left across the corner to a wall-stile. Head up the adjacent field on a right diagonal to a squeeze-stile

Gouged by surging meltwaters at the end of the Ice Age, the spectacular **How Stean Gorge** is over 70ft (21m) deep. A path twists through the narrow defile, where you can wonder at the fantastic shapes that have been sculpted from the rocks and see the surprising range of plant life it supports. There are caves to explore as well, and if you forget your torch, you can hire one at the entrance.

in the top wall and continue climbing on the same course across subsequent fields, eventually reaching a gap breaking a stand of conifers.

Across Nidderdale to Middlesmoor

B Through the trees, resume your former line, climbing towards the buildings of Middlesmoor, which now become visible ahead. From a final gate, a track leads into the village. After passing a tearoom, Dovenor House, and then St Chad's, you will come out opposite the Crown Hotel.

C Turn left down the hill and out of the village. Just after a sharp left-hand bend at the bottom, leave through an opening into the field on the right and follow its boundary away from the road. Continue down the next two fields until you reach a squeeze-stile in the wall on the right. Instead of going through, turn left and cross to the right-hand of two gates in the far wall.

Keep going over subsequent fields until, beyond a gate by a barn, you go down through another gate on the right. The entrance to How Stean Gorge (admission charge) lies ahead, over a bridge at the bottom, spanning the foot of its miniature canyon.

D Walk out onto the lane and go left, following it above the tail of the gorge to a junction. Turn left over a bridge and then right at a second junction back to Lofthouse. Once in the village, you will find the Crown Hotel and car park at the starting point off to the left.

The consecration of **St Chad's Church** in 1484 by the Archbishop of York is well recorded, but claims that a church was here long before then are supported by the age of the font, believed to be Anglo-Saxon. Parts of a cross, said to have been erected by St Chad, were found in the churchyard. He was Bishop of Lichfield in the 7th century and is believed to have preached here whilst on one of his missions.

14 Kirkby Malham to Airton

From Kirkby Malham, whose church has been described as the 'Cathedral of the Dales', this walk wanders across infrequently traversed green pastures to the peaceful hamlet of Airton. Of interest there is a Quaker Meeting House, squatter's cottage and one-time mill. The return allows a leisurely amble along meadows beside the meandering River Aire.

START Kirkby Malham

DISTANCE 4¼ miles (6.8km)

TIME 2 hours

PARKING Parking area by the church

ROUTE FEATURES Moderate climb at beginning of walk; stiles

Rebuilt in the 15th-century Perpendicular style, the **Church of St Michael the Archangel** claims origins in the 9th century from the settlement's name, Kirkby, Scandinavian for 'place with a church'. Its clerestory windows and spacious interior do indeed suggest a cathedral and it contains many interesting features. Some impressive 15th-century box pews, a three-decker pulpit and an ancient triple-lock chest are things to look for and, notice behind the door, a massive wooden bolt to bar it shut when the villagers fled here for safety from raiders. Have a look too for the **'watery grave'** behind the church.

? *What is carved on the second pillar of the south aisle of St Michael's Church?*

From the parking area opposite St Michael's Church, a path (signposted to Otterburn) dips across Kirkby Beck before rising to a field above the gorge. Cross to a stile on the right and then, bearing slightly left, walk up towards a wood at the top corner. After climbing over another stile, continue walking up alongside the trees.

PUBLIC TRANSPORT Bus service from Skipton

REFRESHMENTS Victoria pub in Kirkby Malham (children welcome)

PUBLIC TOILETS Nearest public toilets at Malham

ORDNANCE SURVEY MAPS Explorer OL2 (Yorkshire Dales – Southern & Western areas), Landranger 98 (Wensleydale & Upper Wharfedale)

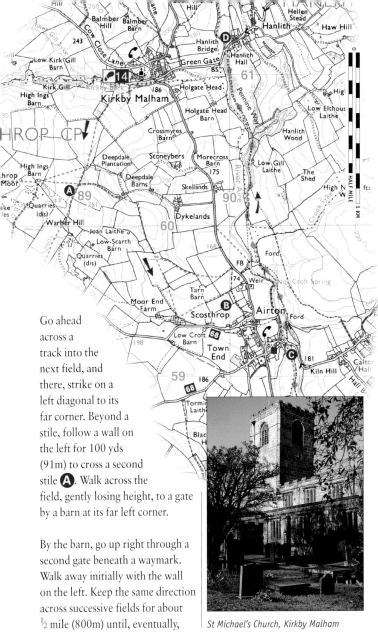

Go ahead across a track into the next field, and there, strike on a left diagonal to its far corner. Beyond a stile, follow a wall on the left for 100 yds (91m) to cross a second stile **A**. Walk across the field, gently losing height, to a gate by a barn at its far left corner.

By the barn, go up right through a second gate beneath a waymark. Walk away initially with the wall on the left. Keep the same direction across successive fields for about ½ mile (800m) until, eventually,

St Michael's Church, Kirkby Malham

you approach barns at Moor End Farm.

However, instead of crossing a fence-stile behind the barns, turn left across the field, parallel to an overhead power line. Then, over a ladder-stile carry on beside a wall on the left until, just past a gate, you reach a stile **B**. Turn right, cross to a ladder-stile on the far wall and continue over the remaining fields. You will finally emerge beside cottages onto a lane at Airton.

At a junction, just to the right, turn sharp left and then immediately right onto a track (signposted Town End), leaving the road between the drives of two houses.

Follow it behind the modern part of the village to another lane. There turn left and walk down to a junction on the main road.

Carry straight over (signposted Calton) beside the village green, down to the Aire **C**. Across the bridge, double back left and go over a stile into a meadow by the river (signposted Pennine Way). The route picks its way along the riverside pastures, shortly crossing a footbridge spanning a side stream, Crook Syke.

Hanlith Bridge across the River Aire

Over the footbridge, bear right and continue following the main river upstream. After one mile (1.6km), a final stile leads onto a lane near Hanlith Hall **D**. Turn left, cross the Aire and walk up the lane for ½ mile (800m), back to Kirkby Malham.

Grassington to Grass Wood

15

Grassington's popularity diminishes none of its character and it is an interesting start for this easy walk to Grass Wood. One of many sites of local prehistoric settlement, the woodland sustains a rich variety of animal and plant life and is particularly beautiful in spring and early summer. The circuit is completed by a relaxing amble along an attractive stretch of the River Wharfe.

START National Park Information Centre outside Grassington

DISTANCE 5 miles (8km)

TIME 2 hours

PARKING Car park beside Information Centre (Pay and Display)

ROUTE FEATURES Generally clear paths and tracks

Go left from the car park towards Grassington and, at the village, turn right into Main Street. Climb past the shops to the top of the town **A** and bear left by the Devonshire Institute into Chapel Street towards Town Head. After 275 yds (252m), turn right onto a track, Bank Lane, and, following signs for Dales Way and Grass Wood Lane, walk up to and go through a hand gate on the left, where the track forks **B**.

Bear right across a field to climb a waymarked stile, then head left to

At the bottom of Grassington, overlooking the square, two former **miners' cottages** house a fascinating museum giving an insight into the life, industry and natural history of the dale.

? *Returning by the Wharfe to Grassington you will see a couple of weirs across the river. What were they for?*

PUBLIC TRANSPORT Bus services from Skipton, Hebden and Leeds

REFRESHMENTS Café within Information Centre and a choice of cafés and pubs in Grassington

PUBLIC TOILETS Adjoining car park

ORDNANCE SURVEY MAPS Explorer OL2 (Yorkshire Dales – Southern & Western areas), Landranger 98 (Wensleydale & Upper Wharfedale)

Native Britons once farmed the surrounding hills and, although not easily identifiable to the untrained eye, the slopes above are littered with remains of **Iron Age settlements** and field systems. Throughout the medieval period the town remained an important centre and was granted a market charter as early as 1282.

another stile. Cross a track from the farm to a wall stile opposite from which you are directed along a right diagonal down a sloping field towards Grass Wood. A stile at the bottom corner leads out on to a walled track.

Walk ahead past barns to the end of the track and pass through the right-hand gate. Keep going along the edge of a narrow field and then bear right across the next enclosure to a ladder-stile into

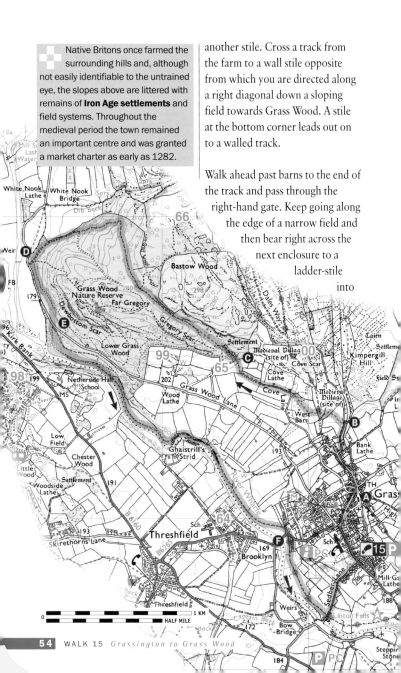

Once the site of an Iron Age encampment, and more recently exploited as a timber resource, **Grass Wood** is now managed to benefit local native varieties of both tree and plant life. The increasing variety of species makes it a delight, particularly in spring when woodland birds and flowers make their appearance.

In 1766 the wood was the scene of a **foul murder**, when Tom Lee, the local blacksmith, but apparently a scoundrel, waylaid a Dr Petty who had threatened to expose him. To cover his tracks, he disposed of the body in the river at Loup Scar. Although twice acquitted of the charge, he was finally convicted on the evidence of a former apprentice and was hanged at the entrance to the wood.

Grass Wood, once the site of an Iron Age encampment.

C Ignore side tracks as you follow an occasionally waymarked, twisting

At the edge of Grass Wood

trail. It climbs through the trees and levels as a surfaced path. At a junction, keep ahead, signed towards Grass Wood Lane, but at a waymark just beyond, fork off right onto a dirt path. Keep going as it descends, later swinging sharply left and running on to rejoin the gravel way.

D Just before a gate out of the wood, turn left onto an unsurfaced path climbing above Grass Wood Lane. Just beyond the crest, where a path joins from the left, look for a fainter path on the right, which drops to a stile out to the lane. Go through a kissing-gate opposite into the lower half of the wood.

Ghaistrill's Strid, above Grassington

E A path through the trees (signposted Grassington) leads to the Wharfe, where it continues downstream. After leaving the wood, the way remains by the riverbank,

With the arrival of the turnpike in the 18th century, the develop-ment of lead-mining on the moors and the conversion of local mills for the textile industry brought a new wealth to Grassington. The boom continued until foreign imports slashed the price of lead, and steam rendered the water mills unable to compete. However, **the local economy** found a new avenue in the arrival of the railway in 1901, which heralded the birth of a tourist industry.

passing through a succession of waterside meadows. Approaching a bridge, bear left over the final field and climb to the road.

F Cross over to a gap in the opposite wall, through which a path drops back to the riverside meadows (signposted Hebden and Burnsall). Keep going downstream until you reach a footbridge, bringing a path across the river from Linton. Now turn left onto a walled, paved path, Sedber Lane, and follow it up the hill and back to the car park from which the walk began.

Along Wharfedale past The Strid to Barden Tower

START Cavendish Bridge, Bolton Abbey

DISTANCE 5¼ miles (8.4km)

TIME 2¾ hours

PARKING Car park below Cavendish Memorial (charge)

ROUTE FEATURES Riverside and woodland walk

16

A deservedly popular walk revealing some of Wharfedale's indisputable charms. Spectacular viewpoints punctuate the undulating upstream woodland walk, which culminates at Barden Tower, a medieval forest lodge. Returning beside the river, the walk winds through Strid Wood, which is noted for its wealth of plant- and wildlife and is especially enchanting in spring and early summer.

Cross the River Wharfe by the footbridge opposite the Cavendish Pavilion and Information Centre and then immediately turn left to follow a path upstream on the opposite bank. Farther on, over a stile, take the lower path, which

> *How many different types of trees and wild flowers can you find in the woods? (Remember that it is illegal to pick wild flowers.)*

Ever since the 19th-century, when the Revd Carr of Bolton Priory Church laid out paths and established viewpoints, **Strid Wood** has been a popular haunt. Predominantly sessile oak (distinguished from the English oak by not having stems to its acorns), its spring carpet includes snowdrops, bluebells and wood anemones. The air is often filled with bird song and you might see nuthatches and tree-creepers in the branches, or dippers and wagtails amongst the riverside rocks.

PUBLIC TRANSPORT Bus services from Ilkley and Leeds

REFRESHMENTS Cafés near car park and at Barden Tower, picnic tables near the Pavilion Café and The Strid

PUBLIC TOILETS Adjoining café and information centre

ORDNANCE SURVEY MAPS Explorer OL2 (Yorkshire Dales – Southern & Western areas), Landranger 104 (Leeds & Bradford)

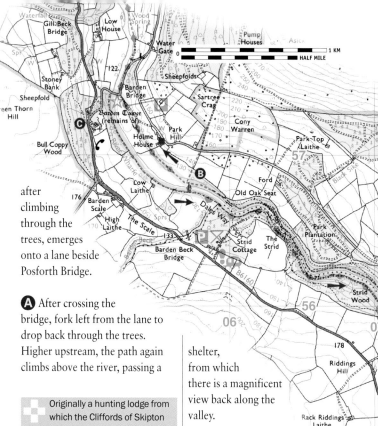

after climbing through the trees, emerges onto a lane beside Posforth Bridge.

A After crossing the bridge, fork left from the lane to drop back through the trees. Higher upstream, the path again climbs above the river, passing a shelter, from which there is a magnificent view back along the valley.

Originally a hunting lodge from which the Cliffords of Skipton Castle administered their forest estates, **Barden Tower** also served to protect local people from harassment by the raiding Scots. In the early 16th century it became the home of Henry Clifford, dubbed the '**Shepherd Lord**' due to his upbringing in exile on a Cumbrian farm. He preferred a simple existence here to the ceremony of court life at the castle. Although abandoned after his death in 1523, it once again became an occasional residence of the Cliffords after its restoration in 1658 by the spirited Lady Anne.

Beyond, the path maintains a high route above The Strid, giving a dramatic perspective over the river's constriction through a narrow cleft in the bedrock. You will get an opportunity to see it at close quarters during the return section of the walk. As you continue, occasional benches beside the path mark some of the most spectacular viewpoints along the valley.

Although barely 6ft (1.8m) wide at its narrowest, the underwater chasm is some 30ft (9.1m) deep, and the roaring torrent has claimed many a life from those foolhardy enough to attempt the leap across **The Strid**. Legend has it that a son of the de Romilles, Norman founders of Skipton Castle, lost his life there during a hunting expedition. In his memory, his mother gave land by the Wharfe to Augustinian canons, on which they founded nearby Bolton Priory.

B *To shorten the walk, you could cross the river here to join the return route, but you would then miss Barden Tower, which lies about ½ mile (800m) farther on.* Continue on this bank along riverside meadows, finally emerging onto a lane beside the next bridge upstream. Go over the Wharfe and walk up the hill until you reach a stile on the left, shortly before a junction at the top. Barden Tower stands just across the field.

C Return towards the bridge but, just before it, leave the road through a squeeze-stile on the right and follow a path on the river's western bank back downstream. Shortly, beyond the aqueduct, a footbridge takes the route over a side stream into Strid Wood.

The Strid

Shortly, the way falls, eventually leaving the wood and rejoining the riverbank by a stone bridge. This is actually an aqueduct, which carries water pipes over the river.

The ruins of Barden Tower, a medieval hunting lodge

Ignore tracks off to the right and, after the path rises past a viewpoint, choose the lower route at a fork for the best views of the river. At another split farther on, again bear left to drop to a large, rocky platform by the water.

Farther downstream, the path again divides. Fork left to follow the river down to Ludstream Islands and a bird hide overlooking the water.

Then go back to the fork and take the other branch, which climbs through the woodland above the islands before returning you to the information centre and car park, just a little farther downstream. ●

Reeth to Marrick Abbey

START Reeth
DISTANCE 6 miles (9.7km)
TIME 3 hours
PARKING Car park above village and around the green (honesty box)
ROUTE FEATURES Sustained climb along a quiet lane during first part of walk; narrow stiles; field paths and tracks may be muddy

17

From Reeth, above the confluence of the Arkle and Swale, hillside pastures give wonderful views along the valley. An idyllic woodland pathway leads on to the former nunnery at Marrick and the return is an easy ramble above the River Swale. Call at St Andrew's in Grinton, the 'mother church' of Swaledale, or visit Reeth's fascinating museum of Swaledale life.

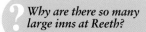 Leave the village green by Ivy Cottage Tea Room, passing the Arkleside Hotel before dropping to the right. At the bottom, by Arkle House, turn right onto a path beside Arkle Beck. Downstream, just beyond a bridge, loop back to reach the road and turn right across the river.

? *Why are there so many large inns at Reeth?*

After bending in front of a garage, go left through a waymarked gate. Bear right across the corner to a gate into the adjacent field and carry on in the same direction to another gate in a projecting wall corner. Through the gate, continue up by the right-hand wall over successive fields, finally joining a lane.

Walk ahead to High Fremington and there, at a junction, turn left to

PUBLIC TRANSPORT Bus service from Leyburn
REFRESHMENTS Choice of pubs and tearooms in Reeth, and the Bridge Inn (bar meals) at Grinton
PUBLIC TOILETS Overlooking village green at Reeth
ORDNANCE SURVEY MAPS Explorer OL30 (Yorkshire Dales – Northern & Central areas), Landranger 98 (Wensleydale & Upper Wharfedale)

climb in front of a cottage **Ⓐ**. Immediately beyond, take a marked footpath beside it, but where that bends behind the cottage, go forward through a stile into the corner of a field. Carry on across successive fields to emerge over a final stile onto a lane.

The climb to the left through a wood is quite steep in places.

The Nun's Causeway through Steps Wood

Levelling beyond Reels Head, the lane bends sharply left. There, at a waymark, go through the second of two gates on the right and walk away beside the right-hand wall.

Ⓑ Carry on across the fields until, after passing beneath a power line, you reach a stile on the right. Cross and continue down on the opposite side of the wall. A final stile leads

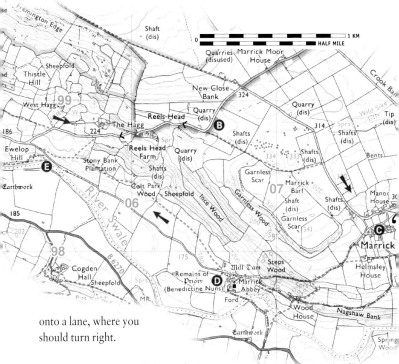

onto a lane, where you
should turn right.

The easy descent towards Marrick
offers splendid views across
Swaledale. At the bottom, where
the lane bends left into the village
above a small green, bear right
down to a farm and turn right
again **C**.

Follow the track to its end and
carry on through a gate down the
ensuing fields, going ahead
through a small yard by a barn,
part way down. In Steps Wood, an
old flagged path maintains the
steady descent, which continues
beyond down a final field. A gate

opens onto a metalled
track at the bottom, which to the
right, leads past Marrick Abbey.

D You could simply follow the
track for the next mile (1.6km).
However, for better views, as you
leave the farm, bear right below an
abandoned corrugated hut through
a gate. Walk across the middle of
this and the next two fields. Then,
over a ladder-stile, follow a fence
and subsequent wall on your left,
eventually crossing it by a squeeze-
stile.

The riverside path follows the Swale to Grinton

Keep the same direction across the remaining fields. Finally, in a more open field, bear left, dropping to rejoin the track from Marrick Priory over a stile. Turn left and walk back 50 yds (46m) to a stile on the right **E**. The path follows the Swale ½ mile (800m) upstream to a road at Grinton Bridge.

F Cross to a gap opposite, from which a faint path bears right, over the fields to a farm by Arkle Beck. Follow a path upstream and carry on along the road beyond its end to recross Reeth Bridge. You can then either retrace your outward steps beside the river or continue up the road into the village back to the starting point. ●

Founded in the 12th century by Augustinians, St Andrew's at Grinton was known as the '**Mother Church' of Swaledale**, and before St Mary's at Muker was built in the 16th century, served all the villages in the dale. Today's building dates largely from the 15th century and amongst its interesting features is a '**leper's squint**' in the south chapel. Leprosy was not uncommon in medieval England and, to reduce the risk of infection, lepers watched the service through the opening and placed their donations in bowls filled with vinegar. As you enter the church, also look for marks around the doorway, made by medieval retainers sharpening their swords and arrows.

Housed in the former Methodist schoolroom, the **Swaledale Folk Museum** depicts many aspects of Dales life, showing the impact that local industries, such as agriculture, mining and knitting, have had upon social conditions.

Buckden to Hubberholme

18

START Buckden
DISTANCE 5¼ miles (8.4km)
TIME 2¾ hours
PARKING Car park in village (Pay and Display)
ROUTE FEATURES Sustained climb at the beginning of the walk; stepping stones

This is a delightful walk, exploring the terraced limestone countryside of Upper Wharfedale. The ascent of Buckden Rake and leisurely traverse above Cray Gill and Hubberholme are rewarded by superb views along the wide, flat-bottomed valley characteristic of its glacial origins. After passing the lovely old church at Hubberholme, the route concludes with a gentle riverside stroll.

A track leaves through a gate from the northern end of the car park, steadily rising through Buckden Wood along the steep

Once the administrative centre of the Percy's great **hunting forest of Langstrothdale**, it was from Buckden that the forest laws were enforced and where the feudal court presided to set fines and punish infringements, such as poaching. Later, as the monastic estates developed the hillsides as vast sheep runs, the village evolved as an important market for the wool.

valley side above the road to Bishopdale (signposted Cray High Bridge and Buckden Pike). Beyond the trees, the way continues through gates at the edge of open moorland enclosures. Shortly levelling off, it turns its back on Wharfedale and heads into a side valley that holds Cray Gill at its base.

? *How did Buckden get its name?*

PUBLIC TRANSPORT Bus services from Ilkley and Leeds
REFRESHMENTS Café and Buck Inn in Buckden, White Lion Inn at Cray, George Inn at Hubberholme (bar meals)
PUBLIC TOILETS Adjoining car park
ORDNANCE SURVEY MAPS Explorer OL30 (Yorkshire Dales – Northern & Central areas), Landranger 98 (Wensleydale & Upper Wharfedale)

Walk ahead (signposted Cray High Bridge) where a path leaves on the right to Buckden Pike, but ⅓ mile (536m) farther on, go through a gate in the wall on the left (signposted Cray). A path, initially quite steep, picks its way down the terraced hillside to a gate at the bottom right-hand

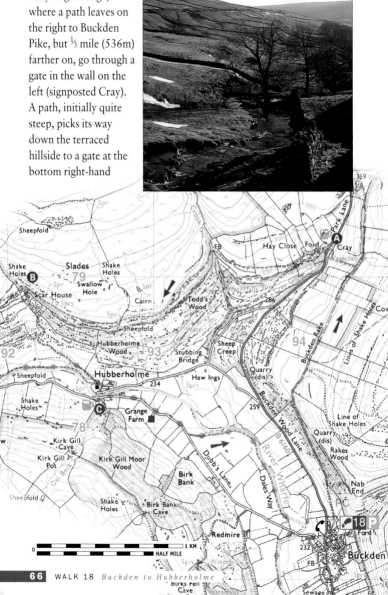

The terraces of Buckden Moor above Cray Gill

corner of the enclosure. Stepping stones take the route across the river beyond, onto a lane opposite the White Lion.

A Directly opposite, a track leads behind the inn (signposted Stubbing Bridge and Yockenthwaite). Bear right up to a barn and go forward through a gated yard. The path leads past more buildings, soon reaching a signpost. Keep straight on passing through a gate towards Scar House and Yockenthwaite.

The way continues ahead through a succession of enclosures, shortly leading over a footbridge above a stream, Crook Gill. On the far bank, go left following a fence line above the steep slopes of Todd's Wood. A mile (1.6km) of easy walking eventually brings you to a junction above Scar House **B**.

The teachings of George Fox found a chord in the independence of the Dales people, and his ideas that became **Quakerism** flourished amongst these isolated settlements. Despite the persecution that was visited on members of the sect, James Tennant of Scar House welcomed Fox to his home in 1652 and 1677. However, his support for the movement landed him in prison at York, where he subsequently died for his beliefs.

The **upper reaches of Wharfedale** were first settled by Norse sheep farmers, who wandered here from the north and west. Their homesteads later became the lodges of the Norman hunting chase and survive as hamlets bearing Scandinavian names such as Cray and Yockenthwaite.

Turn left onto a track (signposted Hubberholme), which drops past the house and continues along the side of the valley.

After joining the Dales Way at the bottom, the route winds around Hubberholme church before leading out onto a minor lane at the end. Turn past the entrance to the churchyard and cross a bridge over the River Wharfe to a junction in front of the George Inn.

C Follow the lane to the left for almost ½ mile (800m), where you can then leave through a gate on the left. A path which is signposted to Buckden Bridge follows the field perimeter down to the Wharfe before winding pleasantly beside the river towards Buckden.

When you get to the final field, before reaching a bridge, cut across it to return to the lane, following it over the River Wharfe and then back to the starting point in the village. ●

19 Settle to Victoria and Jubilee Caves

START Settle

DISTANCE 5¼ miles (8.4km)

TIME 3 hours

PARKING Greenfoot car park (Pay and Display)

ROUTE FEATURES Sustained climb at beginning of walk on track and field paths

Above the cliffs, once perceived to threaten the town with destruction, a wild, moorland landscape is backed by the stark, dramatic crags of Attermire Scar. After traversing its base, a gentle descent above the Ribble gives ample opportunity to enjoy some fine views and, back in Settle, you might end the day with an exploration of the town.

Climb the lawned bank behind the car park onto Commercial Street. Go left to a junction and then right up Albert Hill (signposted Kirkby Malham and Airton). Where the street forks, continue ahead along Greenhead Lane (signposted Pinfold) and, beyond some cottages, bear left before a small picnic area onto a gravel track (signposted Lambert Lane).

As the last Ice Age retreated, small groups of people began to settle the hill slopes, often choosing **caves** as convenient shelters. Excavations in Victoria Cave, so named for its discovery in the year of the Queen's coronation, have revealed flints and bone tools, as well as the remains of several types of animals. There was also evidence that the caves were used during the Roman period, perhaps by bands of native Britons hiding from the invading forces.

Penny Bridge

PUBLIC TRANSPORT Bus and rail services from Skipton

REFRESHMENTS Choice of cafés and pubs in Settle, picnic area above Upper Settle as route leaves the town

PUBLIC TOILETS In Settle's market square

CHILDREN'S PLAY AREA Above car park at start of walk

ORDNANCE SURVEY MAPS Explorer OL2 (Yorkshire Dales – Southern & Western areas), Landranger 98 (Wensleydale & Upper Wharfedale)

At the top of a steep climb, by the entrance to Settle High Reservoir, cross a stile and continue up the left-hand field edge. Turn right along its upper boundary to a gap in the far corner. With the main climb now over, cross into the adjacent field and walk beside its right-hand wall to a ladder-stile, 40 yds (37m) along. Over that, follow the wall on your left

around the perimeter, over a stile into the next field, and eventually out through a gate onto a walled track, Lambert Lane.

A Go left to a lane at its end and turn right. Then, at a bend

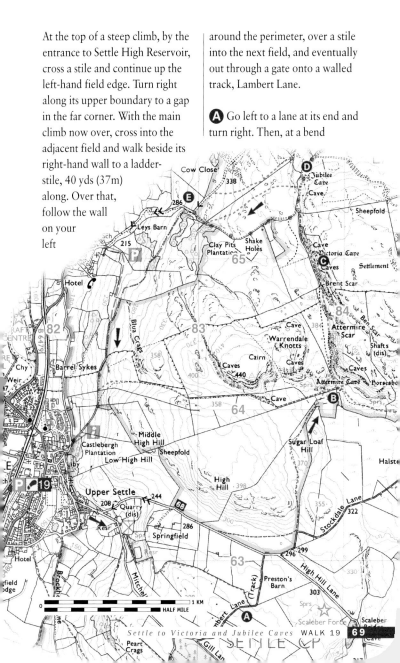

100 yds (91m) on, bear left along a metalled track, Stockdale Lane (sign-posted to Malham). After 200 yds (183m), at a sharp right-hand turn, go ahead over a ladder-stile and up a gravel track (sign-posted to Attermire Scar). Over the crest, where the gravel ends, continue on a green path, passing left of Sugar Loaf Hill.

High cliffs, or scars, mark the line of the Craven Fault

Towards the far end, make for the right-most of two gates and then bear right to walk down a narrowing field to a stile at its bottom. Cross to another stile opposite and, over that, turn right (signposted Highside Lane).

B Then, bear left onto a faint path, climbing through a break in the higher ground above to follow a wall. Cross it at a stile, and continue ascending on its opposite side, below Attermire Scar, which now rises steeply on your right.

Shortly, having diverged from the wall, the gradient eases and the path follows the base of the scree below the cliff. Later, after crossing a stile, the path passes below Victoria Cave **C**. *You are now advised not to enter because of the danger of rock falls.* Eventually, after a second gate at the northern end of the scar, the path drops to a track. Turn right and walk up to Jubilee Cave, which lies to the right of the track, 200 yds (183m) along.

D After looking around, go back 100 yds (91m) down the track to a ladder-stile on the right and cross into a large enclosure. Walk directly away from the wall and ahead over a crossing path, following a faint path down the gently descending hillside. Dropping to a gravel track at the

? *Look for a strange sign on Ye Old Naked Man café, opposite the market square in Settle. What does it mean?*

far end, go right over a cattle-grid onto a lane.

E Turn left and immediately go left again through a gate onto a green path (signposted Settle). After following a wall at the edge of a wood, carry on to cross through a second stand of trees in front. The way continues in the same direction over successive fields, falling towards the town, which shortly appears ahead.

Eventually developing as a track and then a lane, the route descends Constitution Hill into Settle. Go left at a junction onto Castle Hill, but then fork right along a paved street towards the centre of town.

With many fine buildings, some dating to the 17th century, Settle is an attractive, bustling market town. **The Shambles**, in the market square, was originally an open market, the arcading and an upper storey being added later. One of the houses overlooking the square was the home of Dr Buck, to which his friend Edward Elgar often came to stay. Nearby is Tanner Hall, with its fine, mullioned façade, built by a local tanner, Richard Preston. He supposedly spent more than he could afford on the building and it became known as **Richard's Folly**.

To return to the car park, go left along High Street and then straight over the next junction, by the Museum of North Craven Life, into Greenfoot car park. ●

Fine views across the Ribble valley on the return section

20 Malham to the Cove, Gordale Scar and Janet's Foss

START Malham
DISTANCE 5 miles (8km)
TIME 3 hours
PARKING Car park south of village (Pay and Display)
ROUTE FEATURES Steep stepped path beside Malham Cove; *slippery (when wet or icy)* limestone pavement; awkward stiles

This walk's justifiable popularity is reflected in its spectacular scenery. Breathtaking views above Malham Cove's huge amphitheatre are a sharp contrast to the narrow confines of Gordale, where a lusty waterfall cascades into the gorge. Lower down, it is the same stream that tumbles picturesquely over Janet's Foss, from which a delightful walk through woodland and meadows returns you to Malham.

From the car park, turn left through the village, going ahead at the junction just past the Buck Inn. After ⅓ mile (536m), beyond the National Trust-owned Townhead Barn **Ⓐ**, go through a gate on the right (signposted Pennine Way). An undulating path leads across the valley fields to the foot of Malham Cove, whose massive amphitheatre dominates the head of the valley.

Ⓑ Having explored the base of the cove, walk back a short way and turn right to climb a steep but well-laid, stepped path to the top of the cliff. Carefully pick your way to the right over the expanse of limestone pavement, above the

? *What was the pool below Janet's Foss used for?*

PUBLIC TRANSPORT Bus services from Skipton and Leeds
REFRESHMENTS Several cafés and two pubs, Listers Arms Hotel and Buck Inn (families welcome) in Malham
PUBLIC TOILETS Adjoining car park and beside Buck Inn
ORDNANCE SURVEY MAPS Explorer OL2 (Yorkshire Dales – Southern & Western areas), Landranger 98 (Wensleydale & Upper Wharfedale)

head of the cove, to a wall at its far
side. Cross it by a ladder-stile, just
a little way back from the cliff
edge.

C Walk away on a right diagonal
up a gently rising hillside. A grass

path develops,
which, after following a
stretch of wall, continues across
an undulating, rock-scarred
landscape before finally emerging
over a stile onto a lane.

D Cross to a kissing-gate, from
which a clear path is signed to
Gordale. After contouring the

The massive amphitheatre of **Malham Cove** is the finest limestone cirque in Britain, rising vertically over 250ft (76m) above its base and extending 1,000ft (305m) around the head of the valley. It is part of the Craven Fault system, which is revealed in the lines of sheer scars that dominate the area.

At one time a waterfall cascaded over its lip, fed by Malham Tarn, 1¼ miles (2km) to the north. The water now falls into a sink, just south of the lake, leaving a fine example of a **dry valley** running to the top of the cove.

The river that reappears at its base, however, is actually from a different source, a stream rising on the moor to the west of the tarn. Malham Tarn's waters, the source of the River Aire, resurge at Aire Head, just south of Malham.

rising ground to the left, the way passes through a small enclosure at the base of a scree-filled gully. Beyond, through a gate on the right, walk diagonally across the field below to another gate, then follow the wall on your left down, finally emerging onto a lane by a bridge over Gordale Beck.

Follow the lane upstream to a bend and there leave through a gate on the left. A path across a meadow beside the beck leads into a gorge below Gordale Scar, taking you to the foot of a waterfall at its head.

E Walk back down the gorge to the lane and turn right, continuing

The dramatic walk into Gordale

Clapper bridge across Malham Beck

past the bridge met earlier. Just beyond a ruined building, 100 yds (91m) farther on, go through a gate on the left, from which a riverside path is signed to Malham. Almost immediately, to the left of the path, is a vantage above Janet's Foss, the main route dropping to a pool at its base.

The way continues beside the beck through a pretty wooded gorge.

Medieval Malham was, in fact, held by two different monastic owners. Land to the west of the river fell under the estates of Fountains Abbey, whilst the settlement on the east bank was owned by Bolton Priory.

Keep going across the valley bottom, with meadows beyond, continuing ahead when you pass a walled track, leaving to the right ½ mile (800m) farther on **F**. Then, after the next field, turn right and follow a clear path back into Malham.

Janet was a **fairy queen**, who lived in the cave beside the foss. Apart from being a delightful waterfall, it is interesting because of its **tuffa** formation. Evaporating water, collecting on mosses around the lip of the fall, leaves behind a residue of fragile limestone, a process similar to that responsible for many formations in caves.

Further Information

Safety on the Hills

The hills, mountains and moorlands of Britain, though of modest height compared with those in many other countries, need to be treated with respect. Friendly and inviting in good weather, they can quickly be transformed into wet, misty, windswept and potentially dangerous areas of wilderness in bad weather. Even on an outwardly fine and settled summer day, conditions can rapidly deteriorate. In winter, of course, the weather can be even more erratic and the hours of daylight are much shorter.

Therefore it is advisable to always take both warm and waterproof clothing, sufficient nourishing food, a hot drink, first-aid kit, torch and whistle. Wear suitable footwear such as strong walking boots or shoes that give a good grip over rocky terrain and on slippery slopes. Try to obtain a local weather forecast and bear it in mind before you start. Do not be afraid to abandon your proposed route and return to your starting point in the event of a sudden and unexpected deterioration in the weather. Do not go alone. Allow enough time to finish the walk well before nightfall.

Old field patterns can be seen in the terracing around Gordale (Walk 20)

Most of the walks described in this book do not venture into remote wilderness areas and will be safe to do, given due care and respect, at any time of year in all but the most unreasonable weather. Indeed, a crisp, fine winter day often provides perfect walking conditions, with firm ground underfoot and a clarity that is not

A narrow street in Dent leading to Dentdale (Walk 1)

possible to achieve in the other seasons of the year. A few walks, however, are suitable only for reasonably fit and experienced hill walkers able to use a compass and should definitely not be tackled by anyone else during the winter months or in bad weather, especially high winds and mist. These are indicated in the general description that precedes each of the walks.

Follow the Country Code

- Enjoy the countryside and respect its life and work
- Guard against all risk of fire
- Take your litter home
- Fasten all gates
- Help to keep all water clean
- Keep your dogs under control
- Protect wildlife, plants and trees
- Keep to public paths across farmland
- Take special care on country roads
- Leave livestock, crops and machinery alone
- Make no unnecessary noise
- Use gates and stiles to cross fences, hedges and walls

(The Countryside Agency)

Useful Organisations

Campaign to Protect Rural England
128 Southwark Street,
London SE1 0SW
Tel. 020 7981 2800
www.cpre.org.uk

Council for National Parks
6/7 Barnard Mews,
London SW11 1QU
Tel. 020 7924 4077
www.cnp.org.uk

Countryside Agency
John Dower House,
Crescent Place,
Cheltenham, Gloucs. GL50 3RA
Tel. 01242 521381
www.countryside.gov.uk

English Heritage
Customer Services Department,
PO Box 569, Swindon SN2 2YP
Tel. 0870 333 1181
www.english-heritage.org.uk

English Nature
Northminster House,
Peterborough PE1 1UA
Tel. 01733 455000
www.english-nature.org.uk

National Trust
Membership and general enquiries:
PO Box 39, Warrington WA5 7WD
Tel. 0870 458 4000
www.nationaltrust.org.uk
Yorkshire Regional Office:
Goddards, 27 Tadcaster Road,
Dringhouses, York YO24 1GG
Tel. 01904 702021

Ordnance Survey
Romsey Road, Maybush,
Southampton SO16 4GU
Tel. 08456 05 05 05 (Lo-call)

Public transport
National Rail Enquiries
www.nationalrail.co.uk

Traveline
Tel. 0870 6082608
www.traveldales.org.uk
www.dalesbus.org
www.dalesrail.com

Ramblers' Association
2nd Floor, Camelford House,
87–90 Albert Embankment,
London SE1 7TW
Tel. 020 7339 8500
www.ramblers.org.uk

**Yorkshire Dales National Park
Authority**
Yorebridge House, Bainbridge,
Leyburn, N. Yorkshire DL8 3EE
Tel. 0870 166 6333
Colvend, Hebden Road,
Grassington, Skipton, N. Yorkshire
BD23 5LB
Tel. 0870 166 6333
*National Park Authority
visitor centres:*
Aysgarth Falls: 01969 662910
email: Aysgarth@ytbtic.co.uk
Clapham: 01524 251419
email: Clapham@ytbtic.co.uk
Grassington: 01756 752774
email: Grassington@ytbtic.co.uk
Hawes: 01969 667450
email: Hawes@ytbtic.co.uk
Malham: 01729 830363
email: Malham@ytbtic.co.uk
Reeth: 01748 884059
email: Reeth@ytbtic.co.uk
Sedbergh: 01539 620125

Yorkshire Tourist Board
312 Tadcaster Road,
York YO24 1GS
Tel. 0870 609 0000
www.yorkshirevisitor.com

Local tourist information centres:

Bedale: 01677 424604
Horton-in-Ribblesdale:
01729 860333
Ingleton: 01524 241049
Kirkby Stephen: 01768 371199
Leyburn: 01969 623069
Pateley Bridge: 01423 711147
Richmond: 01748 825994
Sedbergh: 015396 20125
Settle: 01729 825192
Skipton: 01756 792809

Youth Hostels Association
Trevelyan House,
Dimple Road, Matlock,
Derbyshire DE4 3YH
Tel. 01629 592600
www.yha.org.uk

Ordnance Survey Maps
Explorers
OL2 (Yorkshire Dales – Southern
& Western areas)
OL30 (Yorkshire Dales – Northern
& Central areas)

Landrangers
98 (Wensleydale & Upper
Wharfedale)
99 (Northallerton & Ripon)
104 (Leeds & Bradford)

A rocky dry riverbed provides a short scramble through Conistone Dib (Walk 7)

Answers to Questions

Walk 1: Fossilised shells of creatures that inhabited the warm carboniferous seas, under which the stone was formed.

Walk 2: It was a tether to which bulls were tied for the cruel sport of bull-baiting.

Walk 3: You'll find an explanation inscribed on the steps leading to the Middle Falls.

Walk 4: It has low walls so as not to impede the panniers carried by the pack animals.

Walk 5: The inscription on the village cross gives the date.

Walk 6: A young cow that has not yet calved.

Walk 7: It is the grid reference of the village. Check it on the Ordnance Survey map.

Walk 8: Look for a plaque on the northern pillar for the date of its construction.

Walk 9 : A pound to hold stray cattle until collected by their owners.

Walk 10: The dale was once called Yoredale after its river, the Ure, but the dale now takes its name from the town of Wensley, 15 miles (24km) downstream.

Walk 11: Three, one on the bank and two standing in the lake.

Walk 12: The source of the River Ribble lies in the moors nearby.

Walk 13: Carved on a drinking fountain in the centre of Lofthouse.

Walk 14: The heads of two children, marking the site of the first village school.

Walk 15: They contained heads of water to drive the water mills at Linton.

Walk 16: Take along a pocket field guide to help you identify them.

Walk 17: The chief town of Swaledale, Reeth held a major market, attracting producers and buyers from miles around.

Walk 18: 'Den' is Old English for valley, thus 'the valley of the bucks or deer'.

Walk 19: The building was once a 17th-century inn, and the name poked fun at the elaborate clothing fashions of the day.

Walk 20: It was used by shepherds who gathered to wash their sheep in it at shearing time.